MW00881787

Love, Faith, and Prayer

Love, Faith and Prayer

Jeffrey A. Daniel

XULON PRESS

Xulon Press
2301 Lucien Way #415
Maitland, FL 32751
407.339.4217
www.xulonpress.com

Paperback ISBN-13: 978-1-6628-4543-7
Hard Cover ISBN-13: 978-1-6628-4544-4
Ebook ISBN-13: 978-1-6628-4545-1

Table of Contents

Dedication

his book is dedicated to God, who I know was, is, and will
be present in all phases of these moving events. There is
also a very special dedication to my lovely wife, Evelyn, all the
prayer warriors, caring relatives, old and new friends, countless
competent doctors, tireless nurses, compassionate therapists, positive patient care assistants, upbeat patient transporters, dedicated
custodians, interested strangers, and many others who prayed for
me through a trying journey in my life.

This book is also dedicated to my mother, who named me
Jeffrey, which means "heavenly peace" according to Universal
Designs, Inc.

On May 6, 2008, Mother gave me a card titled, "Jeffrey,
Heavenly Peace." The Scripture associated with the card was,
"Trust in the Lord with all thine heart; and lean not unto thine
own understanding" (Prov. 3:5).

Coincidentally, my wife, Evelyn, received a similar card from
a friend of hers, where her name means "living light," according
to J-Mar. Both her card and mine referred to the Scripture
Proverbs 3:5.

I was asked to write this book after sharing my story with
several individuals. Every time the story was told, the conclusion

was that we needed to share this with everyone. I am attempting to do that here.

I almost died. It was my God-fearing wife's unconditional *love*, unwavering *faith*, and *prayers* — along with prayer warriors — that thrust me to achieve physical recovery results, which were unimaginable if merely based on science.

Please enjoy, and God bless!

Growing Up Was Fun

"Everything I need to know I learned in Lima, Ohio."

WHENEVER I MEET SOMEONE, I always share that I was born and raised in Lima, Ohio—a small town between Toledo and Dayton, Ohio, right off Interstate 75. I go on to say that Lima is the "hub of the universe!" For me, it was a wonderful place to grow up. We are known for Kewpee™ hamburgers, French fries, and malts.

As a child growing up in Lima, I was always in mischief, from catching praying mantises in large pickle jars to making sure I walked through every puddle on my way home from elementary school. *The Little Rascals* television show had nothing on my group of friends and me. I grew up in the sixties and seventies in Lima, Ohio. I am the youngest of seven children—three brothers and three sisters. People would often think my brother (fourteen months older) and I were twins. I played football from the age of ten through college. I was not very coordinated in my teen years. I was thin but very strong. In high school, I also wrestled for one year (the longest two minutes of my life) and ran track (220, 440, and the one-mile relay). I was considered a scholar athlete. I also sang bass (okay, baritone) in the church choir, where my sister was the choir director and played the piano.

My parents were very supportive of me my whole life. My brothers and sisters gave me both confidence and love; they expected me to be the best I could be in whatever I pursued.

1

I always felt very special growing up. I felt I could accomplish anything,

Over the next few years of my life after high school, I tried to keep myself in good physical and mental shape. My major health issue was suffering from cluster headaches (once or twice a day for months) on an annual and seasonal basis—almost on a routine schedule. For those who may not be familiar with this debilitating illness, I will share with you that, in my experience, a headache would be assigned a rating of three on a scale of one to ten. A migraine might be assigned a rating of six or seven on a scale of one to ten. A cluster headache would be assigned a rating of twenty-eight on a scale of one to ten. During my cluster headache attacks, in a matter of minutes, I would go from being perfectly fine and pain-free to crouched over in a ball with tremendous headache pain just along one side of my head. The cluster headaches presented themselves each year right around the same time during the Thanksgiving holiday when the weather began to change. I was told by the doctors that cluster headaches were triggered by stress; I was initially diagnosed with a possible deviated septum. At the age of twenty-eight, I even had the surgery for a deviated septum with no relief from the annual headaches. Each year, I would get my prescription of anti-seizure medication and steroids. The steroids often made me very hungry—all the time. I would gain twenty to thirty pounds and a few waist sizes each year. One of my work colleagues called me "Fluffy," and my wife called me "Fluffy Cheeks."

College was very challenging. I attended and graduated from the United States Naval Academy in Annapolis, Maryland, where I also played on the football team and ran indoor track. I was not the best football player athletically, but I was very fast (a 4.4-second 40-meter dash). Tragically, in 1983 during my sophomore year of college, I had a major injury during the final blue and gold football scrimmage of that year: a lateral dislocation of my right tibia. My college football injury mimicked that of professional football player Joe Theismann's—without the broken bones or national television coverage, of course. My anterior cruciate ligament (ACL), medial collateral ligament (MCL), and posterior cruciate ligaments (PCL) were all ruptured. I was on crutches for what seemed like forever—I think it was at least one year.

Having attended a Division One school where I played football, I knew I should have been proud and happy, but I struggled with keeping it all together. I was from a small midwestern town and easily distracted. I was a little on the thin side to play a contact sport against powerhouse Division I teams. I was never on the starting offense or defense, but I did play on the special teams. Annapolis focused on academics first. As a college athlete, I had to work very hard to meet the demands of academics and athletics. After my football injury, it took many months for my body to recover, and my life would never physically be the same.

After college and my subsequent years of obligation to the Naval service, I began to work for a Fortune 500 company for many years—decades, even. My civilian (post-military) career afforded me the opportunity to travel all around the world. I visited Israel, Germany, Taiwan, Japan, and Puerto Rico, to name a few. I also traveled to many states in the United States. I met great people in every location. There was always the universal language of a smile and a laugh.

One of my extracurricular job responsibilities at work included the recruitment of college students for internships or co-ops at the company. I met many smart college students from all over the country. However, one of the most impressive co-ops I encountered I met at the local grocery store. One day, I left my work's identification badge on my belt loop when I stopped by the grocery store on the way home from work. The store's cashier noticed my badge and said, "My mom used to work there." The cashier seemed very bright and kind. I asked her what she was doing now. She stated that she was obtaining her electrical engineering degree from Clemson University. I was impressed and let her know that we are always looking for good co-op students and interns at the company where I worked, and she should apply. A few months later she applied, interviewed, and was offered and accepted a co-op position. Well, I can say that after three consecutive successful co-op terms, she was one of the best interns I ever had the pleasure of working with. She went on to finish her master's in engineering and is now doing very well for herself.

I gained tremendous relationships through work along the way. These relationships played a big role in my recovery from the West Nile virus illness. There was not a single day during my three months in the hospital that I either did not have a visitor, letter, or phone call. Those kind gestures meant a lot toward helping in my recovery. The importance of a prayer, card, or phone call went a long way in giving me hope.

The Onset of the Illness

"If you have faith as small as a mustard seed, you can say to this mulberry tree, 'Be uprooted and planted in the sea,' and it will obey you."
Luke 17:6

2011 WAS A VERY MILD WINTER in Cincinnati, Ohio. It was not unusual for me to wear a light jacket that winter versus a heavy winter coat. Some people considered the warm weather a welcomed surprise. However, my thoughts went from gleeful to concerned—especially after fall 2012. During summer 2012, I found several dead birds in my yard. At the time, it seemed a little unusual but not alarming. Now I know that dead birds could be a sign of the West Nile virus in the area, the same illness many in the medical community associated with my condition, which brings me back to the mild 2011 winter. My theory was that due to the mild winter, many of the mosquitoes did not die off as usual, and mosquitoes from the southern United States migrated further north.

In late August 2012, my wife was planning to attend a training class in Cleveland while I stayed home with our young teenage son. On Wednesday, August 22, 2012, I felt I was coming down with flu-like symptoms. I had a mild headache, elevated fever, and tender spine. I thought the headache was associated with the cluster headaches of the past, but it was too early in the season based on my previous cluster headache patterns.

My wife left for Cleveland with a promise from me that I would see a doctor if I did not get any better. Being an obedient husband, later that evening, I went to a local hospital emergency room and presented my symptoms. The emergency room doctor determined I had a viral illness, gave me a prescription for pain killers, and sent me home. I did not feel any better the next day, so I contacted a colleague at work and asked if he could take me to my primary care physician (PCP). My colleague agreed to take me and wait for me. My PCP did not work in the office on Monday, so I saw another doctor who sent me home as well. My wife called from Cleveland every day to check on my progress. I faked it as best I could, but I was often in bed when she called. My wife works in the medical field, so it was difficult to fool her for too long. One day, I woke up in the late evening and told my son to get ready for school—thinking it was the morning. Well, once my wife heard that story, that was enough for her.

Although my wife was due to be at the medical board recertification conference in Cleveland all week, she decided to come home on Wednesday evening, August 29, 2012. After she got home, she insisted that we go to another hospital emergency room on Thursday, August 30, 2012. I walked into the emergency room under my own power, fully oriented, and signed myself in to be checked out by the medical staff.

The next few weeks were a blur. I was admitted to the main hospital floor for observation. I do not remember any of this, but this was how my wife later described it.

The First Blessing –
I Call It a Miracle

"Love can sometimes come across with great passion."

M Y WIFE WAS VERY INTENSE, unusually assertive, and significantly concerned about my wellbeing. I will do my best to capture what I have been told by my wife, Evelyn. (I will give her an opportunity to give her accounts in a later chapter.)

Thank goodness I was in a coma because if I wasn't, I would have made sure I got out of that hospital bed to save my wife from showing her unconditional *love* for me in a very focused and forceful manner. She was intense and seemed to be back in residency. Yes, my wife is a medical doctor. She left no rock unturned. In the emergency room, the doctors needed to do a spinal tap. Of course, my wife was very concerned, and that is when our first blessing occurred. Evelyn called it a miracle. Our first blessing/miracle was that the emergency room doctor on duty was a member of our church, someone whom Evelyn knew personally. The doctor's presence was very calming for Evelyn.

Typically, August is the time of year when new residents begin their training in hospitals. Evelyn was concerned about the experiences of the doctors (i.e., residents) who I would see for treatment; however, the doctor from our church was a very experienced emergency room physician.

There is a nine-day incubation period for the West Nile virus to be detected via a blood test, and that is what they suspected I had.

It was a few days after walking into the emergency room under my own power that I fell into a coma, was placed on a ventilator, and fed via a feeding tube. I was in a coma for approximately fourteen days. After I gained consciousness, I was transferred to another specialty hospital to be weaned off the ventilator.

Now, I must mention that I was in the middle of obtaining my master's degree from local Xavier University. My international coursework included a trip to South America six months prior to this illness occurring. Therefore, at the hospital, I was tested for everything: yellow fever, scarlet fever, and so on.

After only a few days of walking into the hospital, I began to hallucinate. The clouds looked like clowns. While in this hallucinogenic state, I imagined I was at work trying to accomplish certain tasks. A visiting co-worker of mine played along with my illusions while at the hospital. "Get me the status of the project!" I would yell. He would pretend to be a business partner at work who was going to accomplish the tasks I ordered. He would stomp out of the hospital room, slamming the hospital door, only to re-enter and say, "Job accomplished!"

Within a few days, I was placed on a ventilator and fell into a coma. Evelyn called our family and friends. My prognosis looked very grim. Surgeons sawed into my skull to place a shunt in my cranium to relieve potential elevated pressure (encephalitis, swelling of the brain). All I can say is that Evelyn's *love* and *faith* came through loudly and clearly over those next several weeks. Her *love, faith, and prayers* were highly evident by all.

I do not remember much about those first few weeks in the intensive care unit. I was told that all I could do, physically, was slightly move my head to the left. I could not speak at all. My upper extremities did not seem to be affected, but the remainder of my body was weak and basically paralyzed. Eventually, I was given a tracheotomy. I can still remember the awful sucking sound and cringing feeling when the vacuum cleaned out my trachea.

There was one-point when Evelyn told me that she overheard one of the doctors saying they wanted to biopsy my brain to see what was wrong. It was then that my wife said she whispered in my ear (although I was in a coma), "Jeffrey, they are talking about doing some crazy stuff, and you better wake up." She reports that I did wake up within twenty-four hours or so after that whispered talk—thank goodness.

The doctors had to cut my hair to insert the shunt in my skull. The haircut certainly did not fall into the high-fashion category. My hair was cut in a manner resembling a premature balding man where previously I had a full head of hair. I was told my niece said, "I don't think Uncle Jeff will like that haircut..." After reviewing the picture of that haircut a few months later, I hardly recognized myself and agreed with my niece.

One of the nurses on the intensive care floor was born and raised in Lima, Ohio, where I was born. She and my wife prayed together for me every day I was in the ICU. The nurse, being from Lima, gave my wife an extra sense of comfort and kinship.

My wife knew I was making a significant transition in my recovery when I signaled for a piece of paper and pen. I could not talk but signaled for the piece of paper to write. I wrote on the paper, "Short-term disability and American Express," and my wife said, *"He's baaack!"* I still had a long way to go but being concerned about her wellbeing and our family's business affairs meant there was some recognition of who I was prior to the illness.

After reading my note, Evelyn contacted a friend from work and my boss to help navigate the process needed to ensure I had been granted short-term disability from work and that my corporate credit card was current.

What Was Happening Medically

"You will have suffering in this world."
John 16:33

MY ONLY PAST MEDICAL HISTORY of significance included cluster headaches and knee surgery in college.

I presented myself to the hospital following one week of fever and malaise. I was seen by an emergency room doctor on the first occasion, who sent me home. I saw an internal medicine doctor on the second visit, who considered me to be suffering from a viral illness, possibly the flu, and sent me home. On a third occasion, I arrived at the emergency department of yet another hospital on August 30, 2012, with continued malaise and a few days of headaches, with pain radiating down the spine and neck stiffness. I was started on antibiotics and transferred to the main floor. I was allergic to penicillin (I break out in hives). A spinal tap was performed in the emergency room, which revealed elevated protein, decreased glucose, and a lymphocytosis. My course was complicated by a progressively worsening mental status. When first presented, I was alert, oriented, and appropriate. By September 2, 2012, I was developing signs concerning for encephalitis, including word-finding difficulty and hallucinations. Over the day of September 2, 2012, I developed tachypnea with very shallow breathing, tachycardia, hypertension, and intractable hiccups, and my wife was concerned about inflammation along my brain stem. She shared her concerns with the medical staff. I also developed increased nasal secretions that interfered with my breathing. Given my worsening mental status and continued tachypnea, overnight, I was given one dose of medication for a systolic blood pressure of more than 180. On September 3, 2012, I developed bradycardia, irregular breathing, and hypertension. It was recommended that I be transferred to the intensive care unit.

Over the next two days, I clinically deteriorated and was transferred to a step-up for closer observation. I was finally transferred to the ICU for close monitoring of my respiratory status. There was also a concern for Cushing's triad with worsening hypertension (high blood pressure), episodic bradycardia (slow heart rate), and tachypnea (rapid respiration). I had an episode of aspiration (choking on my own saliva) associated with desaturation (low oxygen in the blood). Because I did not improve, the hospital staff repeated my spinal tap in the ICU. I decompensated, and the monitor shot up very high, indicating that I had increased intracranial pressure (swelling of the brain). I was promptly intubated (given an airway tube) and placed on a ventilator. Neurosurgery was promptly called to place an intracranial monitor (IP) inside my brain to monitor the brain's pressure. Everyone was praying. The IP monitor was in place for approximately forty-eight hours. My pressure was never too high, and the monitor was removed.

My cerebrospinal fluid was sent for extensive analysis and viral studies, including the West Nile virus, serologies (blood tests), malignancies, bacterial cultures, autoimmune disorders, fungal cultures, stains, and antigens. All the tests came back as negative, and no specific cause of the meningoencephalitis was discovered after extensive investigation. Evelyn had a hunch that I had the West Nile virus because of the dead birds found in the yard of our home a few weeks/months prior to the start of my illness; she requested (insisted) that I be re-tested for the West Nile virus. I was told there is typically a nine-day incubation period for the West Nile virus. The second West Nile virus test results were inconclusive, but my clinical symptoms and course of illness suggested I had the West Nile virus.

Over the course of the first week, I received a full course of broad-spectrum antibiotics. I received two days of corticosteroids for possible neurosarcoidosis but was stopped when no improvement was observed, and the positive emission tomography (PET) scan was negative for granulomatous disease (an autoimmune disorder). I continued to improve with supportive medical therapy for meningoencephalitis.

It was difficult weaning me off the ventilator. I twice underwent bronchoscopy to obtain cultures and remove the purulent (puss) intra-airway material. Despite improvement in respiratory status, I was unable to tolerate minimal vent settings as necessary for extubation (to get off the ventilator). My hospital course was complicated by stenotrophomanas (bacteria), E. coli, and methicillin susceptible strains staphylococcus aureus (MSSA) pneumonia, which was treated with seven-day and fourteen-day courses of medications.

My hospital course was also complicated by acute renal failure secondary to acyclovir and amphotericin B. The acute renal failure improved with hydration and cessation of nephrotoxic (kidney) agents. At the time of my discharge from the ICU, my creatinine was improved to 1.4 - baseline is less than 1. I also had a mild transaminitis (elevated liver function test) that resolved after a few days, which was attributed to amphotericin B.

My upper extremity weakness was classified as four out of five, and my lower extremity weakness was two out of five. My sensation was intact. Speech therapy was consulted to evaluate me for swallowing and initiation of an oral diet.

Because I could not get off the ventilator, I received a tracheostomy after being intubated (on a ventilator) for two weeks. At the time of discharge to the ventilation rehabilitation hospital, I was afebrile (without fever) for ninety-six hours, leukocytosis resolved (elevated white counts), and chest radiographs (x-ray) improved with marked clinical improvement. The day prior to my discharge to the ventilation rehabilitation hospital, I tolerated nine hours off the ventilator on a tracheotomy collar.

I was to be transferred to Long-Term Acute Care (LTAC) for further ventilator weaning and rehabilitation with physical, occupational, and speech therapy on September 21, 2012. Medication was continued until September 28, 2012, to complete treatment for the E. coli and MSSA pneumonia. My renal function was checked once weekly until labs returned to baseline. If I were to develop fever or worsening pneumonia, treatment with fourteen days of medication was considered to treat stenotrophomanas pneumonia. Medication was used on this admission as a second line therapy due to the acute renal failure. I consistently had tremors and was cold. I lost nearly 30 percent of my body weight.

Day One: September 1, 2012, I was alert and oriented in the morning. Awake most of the night and unsteady on my feet, I had congestion (nasal spray given), was voiding large amounts of urine, bowel movements were loose and brown—not watery, and the specimens were sent to the laboratory. I received ibuprofen and acetaminophen to keep my fever down. Later that day, I had a decline in cognition, Syndrome of Inappropriate Antidiuretic Hormone (SIADH—holding onto water), and increased blood pressure for cortical involvement (swelling on the brain). The magnetic resonance imaging (MRI) showed inflammation consistent with encephalitis (inflammation of the brain). They started fluid restriction and monitored my fluid volume status closely.

Every eight hours, I was checked for renal function and sodium in my urine.

Evelyn was concerned with my mental status and eye movements, stating that my left eye was inward (nystagmus), my right eye was typical, and my heart rate was beating very rapidly. I continued to be disoriented to place and time situations, had inappropriate responses, and was anxious and shaky but able to walk to the bathroom with assistance while running a fever. My wife stayed at my bedside all night.

Day Two: September 2, 2012, I experienced decreased cognition, paranoia, visual hallucinations, trouble organizing eyes, wobbly gait, decreased leg strength, and hiccups.

Day Three: September 3, 2012, I was having appropriate conversations with Evelyn and the nurse. Evelyn was at my bedside for most of the day. I had periods of confused conversation. My Glasgow Coma Scale (GCS) was fourteen. My systolic blood pressure ranged from the 150s to the 170s. My urine output was 2450 milliliters in a few hours. This day continued with neck pain and complaints of double vision. I was transferred to the ICU, bed number five. There was the possibility of Cushing's triad and the setting of two episodes of bradycardia. The neurology department thought it was possible but unlikely because I had no papillary edema in the morning upon my exam. I was given a catheter. There was more confusion and slurred speech.

Days Four: September 4, 2012, I saw a worsening mental status and encephalitis. I was no longer following commands. There were acute events and some episodes of bradycardia (slow heart rate). My eyes rolled back in my head. I became unresponsive but able to mumble words. I had a repeat lumbar puncture (LP).

I was intubated and placed on a ventilator. During the spinal tap, I became more disoriented and started to aspirate (vomit). Acute renal failure occurred. An intracranial pressure (ICP) monitor was placed in my brain.

Day Six: September 6, 2012, I communicated with the nurse by squeezing her hand for "yes." I released her hand on command. Based on squeezes, I was oriented to self, date, and place. I was lethargic but easily aroused, opening my eye to voice and able to track. I was very weak, no spontaneous movement on right lower extremity (RLE), and minimal lower leg movement. I was considered a critically ill patient with a high suspicion of the West Nile versus fungal etiology. I had nonoliguric renal failure.

Day Seven: September 7, 2012, I could move my upper body but was unable to move my lower extremities. No malignant cells were identified. I had continued weakness.

Day Eight: September 8, 2012, included an MRI of my spine. Inflammation around the brain resolved itself, and I was placed on a high dose of steroids. Neurology stated my clinical picture was most likely viral meninencephalitis with associated myositis, myelopathy, radiculitis, and C-spine enlarged. I had no reflexes in my knees, while my ankles and toes were mute. The assessment included possible etiologies for meningoencephalitis, myelopathy, myoclonus with suspected myositis, and radiculitis prior to preservation by history, including viral infection (most likely) but could also include a paraneoplastic autoimmune condition or neurosarcoid. The plan was to agree with high dose steroid burst daily for three days with paraneoplastic autoimmune labs and imaging.

Day Ten: September 10, 2012, I was not responsive.

<u>Day Eleven</u>: September 11, 2012, my mental status significantly improved. There was no sensation in my toes.

<u>Day Twelve</u>: September 12, 2012, I could not move lower extremities. I could move my upper extremities. I failed to get off the ventilator and was scheduled for a tracheotomy consult.

<u>Day Thirteen</u>: September 13, 2012, there was minimal movement in my left foot, and I responded to pain. I also had bilateral knee jerks (343).

<u>Day Fifteen</u>: September 15, 2012, I was deemed a critically ill patient with acute respiratory failure and mental status change.

<u>Day Eighteen</u>: September 18, 2012, a bronchoscopy was performed at my bedside.

<u>Day Nineteen</u>: September 19, 2012, I was given a tracheotomy. Cleaning out the tracheotomy was painful. Although very out of it, I remember this procedure—it gave me the "willies." This procedure happened several times over the next few weeks.

<u>Day Twenty-One</u>: September 21, 2012, I was transferred to a specialty hospital by ambulance to be weaned off the ventilator.

Transfer to New Specialty Hospital

"Pray for me..."

LET'S TAKE INTO ACCOUNT that the metropolitan area of Cincinnati, Ohio, is made up of more than two million people. There are sixteen public schools, several private high schools, and eight major hospitals. There are two major (and several other) universities in the city, with more than tens of thousands of school-aged students. This gives a general assessment of the size of the city.

The day came when I needed to be transferred from intensive care to another specialty hospital, where I could be weaned off the ventilator. I was very weak but conscience. My wife and teenage son were present when the emergency medical service (EMS) transporter asked my teenage son which high school he attended. He replied, "Walnut Hills High School" (WHHS). The EMS driver also graduated from that same high school decades earlier.

The EMS driver went on to tell my wife and son that his daughter graduated from WHHS as well; she eventually graduated from Clemson University with a master's degree in engineering. My wife immediately replied, "Is her name Leigha?"

The driver replied, "Yes." Now, you should know that Leigha was one of the most outstanding engineering co-op students who worked with my team several years earlier. She was very bright with outstanding leadership skills. She once told me that her father was a firefighter. We initially met when she was working as a cashier at the local grocery store. I wore my badge into the store by mistake. She noticed my badge and stated that her mother used to work at the same place. Over the years, I had often talked to my wife about Leigha and how great she was. Who would have ever thought that Leigha's father would be the one to drive me to the hospital that would help wean me from the ventilator?

I remember praying with Leigha's father while on the stretcher. It was comforting to my wife and me to know another one of His blessings had occurred; this was my second blessing. I call it a miracle.

The Third Blessing – I Call It a Miracle

"Be prepared to accept the wonders in life."
Unknown

I WAS ON THE FIFTEENTH FLOOR of a specialty hospital after being transferred from the intensive care hospital. Many of the inpatient censuses in this new hospital were older in age than me. Several physicians, medical assistants, and nurses were there to care for others and me. One person was my rehabilitation doctor; his name was Dr. Wunder. His initial assessment of me was grim. He performed an electromyogram (EMG) on me with little to no response. An EMG is a test where the doctor uses a sharp "needle" with an electrical charge to test my nervous system. In my case, there was no response in my lower body, and that was not good. However, he had been practicing for more than thirty years, and his name said it all: Dr. Wunder! He was very optimistic and encouraging. This was another sign to my wife that everything would be okay. Eventually, I was taken to the inpatient rehabilitation unit in the same hospital. Before I went there, I was asked if I was prepared to exercise twice a day for a few hours. I said, "Yes." After all, I was an athlete. My third blessing (I call it a miracle) was the heartfelt comfort my wife and I had with the kindness and knowledge of a doctor with the ideal, perfect name of Dr. Wunder.

The Fourth Miracle

"My name is *Faith*."

AFTER A FEW WEEKS of running back and forth to the hospital, my wife was exhausted. She had visited the hospital every day—twice per day (before and after work). She was encouraged by our family and friends to take a break. One day, she decided to take a break and get her eyebrows shaped. She went to the local salon for some pampering. The clerk at the counter said, "You seem frazzled; what's wrong?" My wife went on to explain that I was in the hospital, most likely due to the West Nile virus. The clerk shared with my wife that her nephew also had the West Nile virus a few years earlier but was now doing very well, and you would never know he had the virus. My wife said thank you and, "What is your name?" She replied, "My name is *Faith*." My wife got the eyebrow technician's business card because she said no one would believe it. Again, my wife was reassured by God that everything would be okay and to keep the *faith* – our fourth blessing – I call it a miracle.

Nature's Song

*"Look at the birds of the air, that they do not sow, nor reap nor gather
into barns, and yet your heavenly Father feeds them.
Are you not worth much more than they?"*

Matthew 6:26

FOR MANY OF THE NIGHTS that I was in the hospital, my wife would tell me about an owl that would "hoot" outside our bedroom window during the night to sing her to sleep when she went home after her hospital visits. She stated how much she looked forward to that owl's song each night. The owl was huge (approximately one-foot tall). It sat in a tree right outside our bedroom, and sometimes it would sit on the tree house in the front yard. The owl became a sort of a guardian for my wife. Its presence helped put her to sleep at night.

The Fifth Blessing

I Call a Miracle – Literally

A FTER SEVERAL WEEKS on the in-patient high-risk fifteenth floor, I was transferred to the inpatient rehabilitation
unit. As I mentioned, I was a decent athlete. I participated in football, track, and wresting in high school. I thought two minutes
of wrestling was the longest two minutes of my life. Well, that
was until I experienced the two minutes of inpatient physical and
occupational therapy.

I had therapy twice per day. A patient care assistant would help
me transition from the hospital bed to a wheelchair and then wheel
me to the therapy room. I had occupational therapy in the morning
and physical therapy in the afternoon. There were many therapy
exercises, but I only remember a few. One exercise I remember
from occupational therapy was "tall kneeling." This consisted of
pushing my upper body onto the top of a giant rubber ball with
both hands. Now, I was a guy who played college football and
conquered many obstacle courses, but I was having a very difficult time just pushing my torso up onto the top of a big rubber ball
with my hands and arms. No, I did not ask myself the relevance of
tall kneeling—I just did it. I trusted the therapists unconditionally
and with unwavering *faith*. I was very determined to accomplish
the exercises I was asked to complete. Very often, I was unable to
complete the exercises assigned to me. However, the day I finally
achieved one of the exercises on my own was very rewarding.

During each therapy session, I would live in the moment, every minute-by-minute, and every second-by-second. I was not looking ahead, but I was focused on the now! So, where is the miracle in all of this? Well, the very first time I had to be transferred out of the hospital bed I was horrified about leaving the comfort of my hospital bed. The patient care assistant who came to transfer me to the gym was cheerful but a little small. When he directed me to get out of the bed, I pulled myself up and jumped into his arms with a great big bear hug. I had a death grip on him and was not going to let go for anything. Well, this patient care assistant's name was Mr. Miracle.

So, with Dr. Wunder as a Physical Medicine and Rehabilitation doctor and a Patient Care Assistant (PCA) named Mr. Miracle, I knew everything would be just fine. Yes, this was my fifth blessing (I call it a miracle) as God let us know that everything would be fine.

Family

"It takes a village..."

MY WIFE KNEW THE IMPORTANCE of muscle mobility when a person is sedentary. She asked family members to work my joints: fingers, legs, and arms. Evelyn focused on the toes and legs. Family members took shifts moving my joints while I was in a coma—certainly an advantage of having three sisters. One of my sisters is an accomplished pianist. Anyone who plays the piano knows the importance of upper phalange strength. Family members also sent cards (lots of cards) and pictures, so when I looked around the hospital room, I could see and remember the family members and friends who loved me. Their cards and pictures were very comforting and encouraging.

Friends

M Y WIFE ONLY WANTED no more than one hospital visitor per day to ensure I would not get too exhausted and to minimize the opportunity for any infections. She also only wanted positive attitudes to enter my hospital room. She recruited a co-worker friend of mine, Mike, to manage the list of visitors I would see from my work.

Mike came to visit each day during the first phases of my illness. He would often read to me, although I was often in a coma-like state and slept more than I was awake. Evelyn told me that Mike would read to me for hours, and when he thought I was asleep, he would very quietly close the book, only for me to suddenly wake up and say, "So what happened next?" He would then re-open the book and continue reading. Evelyn said this occurred several times, and Mike patiently continued this ritual for hours and days on end.

Another co-worker came and prayed the rosary with Evelyn for hours. Although I do not remember, Evelyn shared the dedication and conviction of this co-worker.

I was a member of a Bible study group prior to my illness, and members of that group also visited, and we prayed together.

One of my co-workers and her husband also prayed over me.

Those who took the time to visit meant the world to Evelyn and me.

Once, when Mike was visiting, I requested a piece of paper where I wrote, "I can't talk!" Mike wrote back to me, "I know." My wife thought that interaction between Mike and me was hilarious; after all, I could hear and Mike could talk, yet we both decided to communicate via handwritten notes. Now, that's a friend.

I even once got a visit from the family dog. My wife said that as soon as the dog was on the hospital floor where my room was located, the dog darted straight for my room. When my wife took my clothes home to wash them, the dog would often bury his nose in the basket as if to say, "Where is Dad?" It was a great day with the surprise visit from the family dog.

In more than three months of being in the hospital, there was not one single day that I went without having a positive visitor experience. What a blessing!

The Sixth Blessing

"Iron sharpens iron, and one man sharpens another."
Proverbs 27:17

I WAS TOLD that another member of our church was stricken by the West Nile virus. Well, the odds were slim but not that remarkable. What was remarkable was that we both drove the exact same vehicles, which, again, may not seem so unusual. However, the vehicles were both eight-year-old, 2006, blue-pearl, Toyota Highlander hybrids with vanity plates. These cars were identical down to the tow hitches in the back. Evelyn had often interacted with this church member for business reasons. I really had to meet this person. Evelyn pointed out his vehicle in the church parking lot one day, and I was in awe. We finally met at the end of mass and had a long conversation about our illnesses.

Jokingly, he and I concluded that the hypothesis of driving a 2006 pearl-blue Toyota Highlander was not the cause of contracting the West Nile virus.

His positive spirit and drive were very encouraging to me. He was walking on his own and running again. I call our meeting the sixth blessing or miracle. It was how God showed me the power of His healing. Let's not forget that we both drove the exact same model and color vehicles (silly, but true).

Unwavering Faith

"Then Jesus told him, 'Because you have seen me, you have believed; blessed are **those who have not seen** and yet have believed.'"
John 20:29 (emphasis mine)

E VERY FEW DAYS in the hospital, I was assisted by the occupational therapists in taking a shower. I had to first transition from my wheelchair to a bench in the shower itself. Oh yes, what a wonderful feeling having that warm water flow over my body. Although it took more than two hours to take a shower, I thoroughly enjoyed every second.

I was also incontinent, so I was eventually taught to catheter myself. Again, I lived in the moment and learned to be more independent. My liquid output was measured each day. If I did not void enough, the nurse would insist I drink more fluids. Sometimes, I would drink two quarts of fluids in a matter of minutes just to keep myself from becoming dehydrated. I had to realize that fluids were my medicine and friend.

I constantly believed in God's grace and mercy and lived in the moment. My *faith* never wavered!

Love (Unconditional)

"But now abideth faith, hope, love, these three;
and the greatest of these is love."
1 Corinthians 13:13

MY RECOMMENDATION to all is this: never let a significant event, such as the one I experienced, keep you from being totally open to the one you *love* and the one who loves you. Remember, God always loves you!

Evelyn would come to visit me twice a day every single day for the three months I was in the hospital. She came before going to work and at the end of her workday. Her dedication, *love*, support, and kindness inspired the entire clinical staff in the hospital. She would often bring special treats for the hospital staff: chocolate, cookies, and thank-you cards. Her unconditional *love* was my seventh blessing (I call it a miracle).

As I continued to recover, my wife would visit daily. Sometimes, she would fall asleep on the end of my hospital bed. She just wanted to be nearby. I would tell her to go home, but she wasn't having it. She would sometimes bring special meals for me to the hospital and always something for the nursing staff, as well. Many of the nursing staff were familiar with my wife as she had worked as a hospitalist in this hospital for many years. We discovered many of the nursing staff lived within a few miles of our residence.

"How did she do it?" I often asked myself that question of my wife. In a matter of days, I went from a strong and virile husband to a person totally relying on her. Neither she nor any of my care-givers made me feel less than a person. Despite my shortcomings and mistakes, I never was made to feel bad but always made to feel like everything was going to be okay.

Faith

*"Trust in the LORD with all your heart and
lean not on your own understanding."*
Proverbs 3:5

SOME PEOPLE WOULD ASK ME, "Do you ever ask,
'Why me?'"

I can honestly say, "No!" I am a miracle—God's miracle! I
feel blessed that I am so much closer to God and His *love* for me
and that I am an evangelist for God without even opening my
mouth. I give a testimony of God's grace, mercy, and *love* by
merely walking around. This illness made my *faith* much, much
stronger, and I would not change a single thing.

Prayer

"Tall kneeling was tough—I needed it to pray."

REMEMBER EARLIER when I shared my struggles with tall kneeling on a huge rubber ball? As I became stronger and stronger, it appeared to me that the tall kneeling exercise was a precursor to being able to kneel and pray. Through my struggles to kneel on the big rubber ball, I gained a significant appreciation for those small things in life that I just took for granted before my illness. My core was, initially, very weak.

As I was continuing my recovery in the hospital, my wife would share how members of the church and children from the church's school were praying for me. They even had a special mass for me. Everyone was encouraged with the progress I had been making. It was people's encouragement that kept me going. I did not want to let anyone down—as well as myself. Friends and strangers would support my wife through encouragement and *prayer*. I became even closer to God's grace and mercy.

Recovery

"Invest in oneself as you would invest in the Lord."
Unknown

RECOVERY WAS ROUGH and tiring. An eighth blessing (miracle) happened in the most unlikely of circumstances. I attended mass at the hospital one day and tried to roll my wheelchair to the altar to receive the host. When I turned down the aisle where everyone else turned to return to their seats, I had a problem. Immediately, I realized I was stuck. My wheelchair was too wide to fit through the narrow aisle. For the first time, I became overwhelmed with emotion. I began to cry openly. Several members attending mass took the time to move chairs out of the way so I could make it back to my spot in the back of the church. At the end of mass, Evelyn and I were transitioning down the hall of the hospital when Evelyn ran into a nurse from the hospital's maternity unit whom she knew.

My wife told the nurse about my story of the West Nile virus. The nurse replied that her neighbor also had a similar illness and was an outstanding person—this was my eighth blessing or miracle. The nurse said, "Perhaps I can let my neighbor know about your situation, and there could be a hospital visit." Yes, this person came to the hospital a few weeks later to visit with me.

He shared some tips, which I remember to this day:

43

1. Don't look at your physical progress on a day-by-day or week-by-week basis; rather, you should look at your physical progress in six-month intervals.

These words really resonated with me because, as athletes, we used the motto, "no pain, no gain;" however, in this West Nile virus journey, that motto was not prudent.

2. When observing someone doing something well in rehab, say to yourself, "I want to do that too." Always strive to set your own personal goals.

This advice was very pertinent during rehabilitation. For example, once there was an elderly gentleman in therapy who was at least thirty years my senior walking on his walker at a much faster pace than me. I was slowly walking and bent over on my walker in pain as he sped by and passed me several times. Instead of getting down on myself, I reflected on the words, "I want to do that too." Sure enough, I was eventually doing that too—many months later.

There were several distinct events that I can recall in my recovery:

1. One day, I looked at my reflection in the hospital glass window and saw a "skeleton," and that skeleton was me. I knew that I needed to eat more. All the positive visitors in and out of my hospital room never said, "Jeffrey, you look like a skeleton," which I appreciated. My mind was made up that food was my medicine.

2. Due to the lack of feeling in my lower legs, I had a terrible time with proprioception. One time on the parallel bars, the physical therapist asked me to let go with one hand. Once I let go with one hand, I just knew that I was

pirouetting on the parallel bars. In my mind, I was performing an Olympic gymnast move. I had no idea my feet were on solid ground. I could not feel my feet.

3. Walking for the first time with borrowed leg braces was scary, but I knew the person who walked on them before had to be one brave soul. I drew strength from the thought of the original owner walking in the same braces. It was a blessing that the person's leg braces I was borrowing fit me perfectly. We were obviously the same size in height and weight.

4. Taking steps on a walker for the first time was scary. Taking my first forty steps on a walker with leg braces was amazing! When first presented with the idea of using a walker, all I could do was imagine how quickly I would fall and how the walker would slip from underneath me. My first attempt at using the walker involved me being bent over and tense while taking two unsteady shuffled steps. The laws of physics seemed to not be in my favor. My therapist said, "You did better than I expected." It was the confidence the physical therapists had in me that gave me the strength to keep going. The therapists believed in me more than I believed in myself.

5. My first visit outside the hospital after months indoors included a trip to a local restaurant. I had to try and roll my wheelchair up a hill. It was during that trip that I knew I never wanted to take a wheelchair up or down an incline (no matter how slight)—especially near a busy street. It was a dangerous and eye-opening adventure.

6. Imagery was very important. Long before I could walk, one of my friends wrote, "Imagine yourself walking." Those words were surely a long way from being in a wheelchair,

but again, I was given words I could visualize. I dreamed of taking that first independent step, and I was glad and blessed when that first step occurred.

7. The first time I felt a drop of water on the top of my feet in the shower, I shared that information with Evelyn. It didn't seem to be a big deal to me at the time, but it was for her. She let the physical therapist know about my new discovery. It meant that my nerves were waking up. Taking my first shower standing up on my own was amazing.

Back to Work

"But Jesus beheld *them*, and said unto them, with men this is
impossible; but with God all things are possible."

Matthew 19:26 KJV

I WENT BACK TO WORK in late February 2013. I had a totally
different perspective on architectural beauty. A ten-foot glass
door no longer seemed pragmatic. Those doors were very heavy
and impractical. Trying to open a ten-foot door in a wheelchair
proved to be a very challenging task. I eventually got a scooter to
get around the campus at work.

There is one comment that sticks with me. One day, I was
trying to eat my lunch of nuts and fruit at my desk in my wheelchair, and I realized that I was making a mess of my cubicle space.
I shared my concern with the person who daily cleaned the cubi-
cles. His pleasant response was, "You do what you do, and I do
what I do!" In essence, he stated, "Don't worry about me, and I
won't worry about you." It was comforting to know he cared, and
we both had jobs to do.

A few of my favorite sayings while zipping around the
campus include:

- While zipping around on my scooter in the halls, I would
  say, "Walking is overrated!"

- Attitude is everything, and I would say to those wishing to lose weight, "I don't recommend tube feeding as a weight-loss program!"

- Living in the moment and trusting in the Lord; if I saw someone frustrated about a mistake, he made, I would say, "If that's the worst thing that happened to me today, then I'd think I was doing pretty good!"

The Wonderful Care Givers

*"The LORD God said, 'It is not good for the man to be alone.
I will make a helper suitable for him.'"*
Genesis 2:18

I NOW REALIZE that there are several different types of clinical and non-clinical rehabilitation caregivers, and each one played an important role in my journey.

First, there is the family member. I was very fortunate to have such a dedicated wife, caring family, new friends, and supportive co-workers

Next, there is the registered nurse. This is a nurse with at least a Bachelor of Science in nursing. He can issue medication and is the right hand to the medical doctor. I have heard it said that the doctor may do the surgery and save your life, but it's the nurses and therapists who keep you alive (and I would add they also enhance your quality of life).

The medical assistants performed all the daily tasks of keeping the patient clean and comfortable.

There was also a role called the patient care assistant, who faithfully took the patient back and forth to the various therapy sessions.

Another role is that of the trusted physical therapist. His training is extensive and to be respected. He understands the body and spirit of the patient.

An occupational therapist prepares the patient for daily living activities. His pragmatic approach is key once the patient returns home.

Speech therapists focus on teaching the patient to talk and use language. I only needed this type of therapist for a brief period.

The cleaning staff are some of the most dedicated and important roles in the hospital. They ensure infections are not spread throughout the hospital.

Clergy staff were essential for me. It was great to get mass daily and pray with the staffer.

Food service personnel are important too! Having been in the hospital for so long, I knew the rotation of the meals.

The phlebotomists usually wake up the patient in the middle of the night. Their role is key and often unappreciated. I always thanked them for their service.

The social worker helped me with handicapped placards for the vehicles, public transit for disabled passengers, and working with the advocate from my insurance company.

Transporters move patients from one department of the hospital to another for appointments and so on; they use such kindness in carrying out their roles.

Front desk personnel sometimes do all the scheduling. They are often the first people the patient's family sees; therefore, they are the first impression and representation of the hospital itself.

Oh, yes, and there is the physical, medicine, and rehabilitation doctor. All I can say is, "Thank you!" Choosing the specialty that he did has enabled me to move through this journey in confidence versus in fear.

Because I had no feeling in my lower extremities, a podiatrist had to clip my toenails. Yes, podiatrists do more than just work on bunions—thank goodness. After I clipped my toenails too short, I learned to really appreciate the skills of the foot doctor.

Facilities personnel take care of the hospital room temperatures and equipment. I would be remis if I did not thank the electricians that maintained the hospital equipment. Thanking those who are often taken for granted is very important to me.

There were many other medical specialties important in the overall support of my journey.

Collectively, the entire clinical and non-clinical team had a hand in making me feel special and assisted in my healing. I may have felt bad about having bathroom accidents, but the clinical team never made me feel ashamed for having accidents. I was pushed and challenged by the staff. What a wonderful and loving group of individuals. All patients were treated with the utmost respect.

Nurses and Therapists Are Special

"Nurses and therapists are special people. They make each individual feel special—no matter what your background is."

I MUST GIVE A SPECIAL shout-out to the therapists and nurses. They were as invested in my recovery and progress as I was. Even more importantly, they knew where I was headed because they had either seen it before or trained to know the process. I fully trusted their opinions, guidance, direction, and support. It was not always easy to adhere to the requests they made, but I always tried. Surprising the nursing staff with a "thank you," donuts, coffee, or candy goes a long way to let them know the family cares and thanks them for the great job they do to take care of their patients every day.

A Warm Blanket

"Jael went out to meet Sisera and said to him, 'Come, my lord,
come right in. Don't be afraid.' So, he entered her tent,
and she covered him with a blanket."

Judges 4:18

A S I MENTIONED EARLIER, when I finally looked in the
mirror, I saw a skeleton—and it was me. I kept my hospital
room in the ninety-degree Fahrenheit range. It was a very special
night when I was given a warm blanket at bedtime. I felt as though
I was wrapped in my mother's arms. Many nights, my wife asked
for me to be given a warm blanket.

Time for a Visit Home

GOING HOME the first time was exciting. Thank goodness, we had a first-floor bedroom and full bathroom. First things first, could my wheelchair fit through the doors? I did not think so. Of course, trying to fit the wheelchair straight through the doorway did not seem to work. So, I had the first-floor interior doors removed and replaced with curtains.

Ah, my first sleep at home for a while... but I shouldn't have been so eager. Our pillowtop mattress was very soft—too soft for a person with a very weak core. I had very little muscle tone and was unable to pull myself up without assistance. As my wife rolled me into the bed, I had sunk into the pillowtop mattress more and more and more. I said to my wife, "Please, roll me over!" Later that week, I had the firm mattress upstairs traded out with the pillowtop mattress. Someone would have to lift my legs onto the bed. I had to sleep with more than ten pillows to elevate my feet to reduce the pain.

After a few months, I discovered that the wheelchair did fit through the doors if I was careful. All those weeks with a curtain on my bedroom door were for naught.

I lost a lot of weight and was always cold. I wanted the entire house to be warmer than eighty degrees Fahrenheit. Unlike some vehicles, which have dual heat for the driver and passenger, a house is either warm or not warm. Electric blankets became my friends, for which my wife was very grateful.

Living One Day at a Time

God's Grace and Mercy

A FTER RETURNING HOME, I began to live one day at a time. I transitioned to outpatient physical therapy three times per week. My wife transported me back and forth to therapy. I was always tired and slept often. I had to motivate myself to motivate others. My wife got a great workout; she had to break down my wheelchair a few times per day and lift it into the back of the car. Evelyn did not complain once about her role as a caregiver. I was very lucky and fortunate.

Giving Back and Paying Forward

ALL THOSE WHO I GAVE my best, both humbly and with grace, gave back to my family and me with *prayers* and good wishes. I look at myself as a living testimony for the grace and humility of God. It was the warm relationships gained and nurtured prior to the illness that came back ten-fold when we needed them most. Yes, I am a miracle! I tell anyone who will listen about my journey, the blessings I have encountered, and the *love* of God!

How Did She Do It?

*"Then Jesus told him, 'Because you have seen me, you have believed; blessed are **those who have not seen** and yet have believed'"*

JOHN 20:29 (emphasis mine).

I AM A MIRACLE! And my wife is an angel. Every day before work and every day after work, my wife would visit me in the hospital. Sometimes I would find her asleep at the foot of my hospital bed. One of the housekeepers put an extra recliner in the room for her comfort. After I got sick, she had to do it all. She paid the bills and got herself and others ready in the morning for school and work.

She developed strong relationships with the clinical staff in the hospital. Everyone began to know how much she loved me. Her *love* and kindness were contagious.

The Ups and Downs

"More than that, we rejoice in our sufferings, knowing that
suffering produces endurance."

Romans 5:3

FROM A WHEELCHAIR to a walker was a significant step.
Going from a walker to a cane was significant but going from
a cane to walking independently was challenging and different
from the previous transitions. Walking unsteadily to walking "normally" would take some time. The more ambulatory I got, the
more I wanted to run.

"Think in six-month intervals," I thought.

Not every moment was upbeat. There were times that I just
wanted to walk "normally" or run. No longer could I depend
solely on Evelyn for inspiration. She worked very hard to make
sure I continued to realize my blessings and how far I had come.
Sometimes, I just wanted some sympathy—but that feeling never
lasted too long.

Previously, it was not unusual for me to arrive at work at 4:00
a.m. and leave after 7:00 p.m. the same day. Working at a different pace was difficult. I wonder if my body's resistance was
low because of pushing myself so hard prior to getting sick. I had
to reevaluate life going forward and my role in it.

The Journey Continues

"More than that, we rejoice in our sufferings, knowing that suffering
produces endurance, and endurance produces character, and character
produces hope, and hope does not put us to shame, because
God's love has been poured into our hearts through the
Holy Spirit who has been given to us."

Romans 5:3–5

MY WIFE GAVE some of our friends and me a postcard
with the Black Madonna on it in 2013. The words that
stick with me the most over my journey of healing are the teach-
ings on mercy and grace. In 2014, there was a Black Madonna tour
going across the United States. We went to see the Black Madonna
at a local church. The back of the Black Madonna card stated, "...
Today, I consecrate myself to Thee, Good Mother, totally—with
body and soul amid joy and sufferings to obtain for myself and
others thy blessings on this earth and eternal life in Heaven... "

I am truly blessed and encouraged when a stranger comes
up to me and says, "Hey, you are no longer on the scooter. Great
for you!" or "You really inspire me!" Certainly, I would think I
would probably be as encouraged taking this journey without all
the encouragement, but I would not like to find out.

I have taken on several additional activities to support my
recovery: acupuncture, massage, vitamins, Pilates, and water aer-
obics. I am investing in "me."

Although very costly, I discovered acupuncture as a com-
pliment to traditional medicine. The medical doctor who gives

me acupuncture treatments had the West Nile virus herself a few months prior to me. Once again, I had found a practice where my wellbeing was as important for the doctor as it was for me—another blessing, another miracle. I initially had treatments every two weeks while on a walker.

I supplement the acupuncture with full body massages—also done every other week. I initially started massage therapy while using a walker. I only had one massage prior to my illness. I had a lot of muscle spasms or tone. By seeing the same massage therapist for several months, she could note any improvements in my body tone. At first, I was not able to bear a deep tissue massage; after several months, a deep tissue massage was tolerated. The massage typically took forty-five minutes. The masseuse would give me extra time in the beginning. Again, this was another individual as concerned about my wellbeing as myself.

Marathon

"The LORD makes firm the steps of the one who delights in him..."
Psalm 37:23

MY ONE-KILOMETER MARATHON team's name was Full Recovery. I walked the total of a one-kilometer marathon just nineteen months after my original illness. Yes, one kilometer equals six-tenths of a mile.

The annual Heart Mini Marathon® in Cincinnati has a one-kilometer race for stroke victims. My wife thought it would be a good idea for me to walk the one-kilometer race. She ran the ten kilometers earlier in the day. It was a very cold day in March 2014. Yet, it was very invigorating to finish the race.

Many of the therapists I had been working with over that year had their own team, the Rehab Racers, and were present for my race too! Finishing that one-kilometer race meant more than finishing any five or ten-kilometer race I had ever participated in before.

March 2014 was nineteen months post my illness. I had gone from the wheelchair to a walker to, primarily, walking with a cane.

I will never forget the feeling of crossing the finish line. I have been on the constant lookout for a bumper sticker that says, "0.6," like the "13.1" and "26.2" car bumper stickers that are readily available.

My next goal was to complete a five-kilometer marathon and, ultimately, a full marathon. It would be a great accomplishment even without my illness.

Inpatient Rehabilitation

"My precious child, I love you and would never leave you. During
your times of trial and suffering, when you see only one set of
footprints, it was then that I carried you."

"Footprints in the Sand" by Mary Stevenson

E VERY DAY I WAS CONFLICTED in participating in
therapy because the sessions wiped me out, but I knew they
were good for me to improve my situation. As I mentioned earlier, I had lost nearly seventy pounds and a lot of muscle mass
through atrophy.

My initial therapy started with just moving my legs on a board
while strapped to what seemed like roller skates. I was asked to
swing my leg forward and backward as best I could. I focused on the
task at hand and trusted my physical therapist. She was so patient.

Although the therapy table was only about one foot off the
ground, it would sometimes take me twenty minutes to swing
my leg up onto the mat table. The physical therapist would sit
patiently and wait as I tried and tried and tried again. She really
focused on me becoming independent. I never thought she was
mean. I trusted that she knew what she was doing. I could tell she
wanted the best for me.

The day I could just swing my leg onto the mat table within a
few seconds gave me such a feeling of accomplishment.

Other memorable exercises included the balance board (left,
right, and in the middle—again and again). The scariest physical

therapy exercise was the treadmill. I often had low blood pressure. When placed in the treadmill's harness to remove 60 percent of my weight or more, I passed out on at least two occasions. Speaking of those outstanding therapists, when I passed out, it was the smallest therapist in the room who grabbed my legs as I sat in the wheelchair and tilted me so my feet would be above my heart.

I did occupational therapy in the morning and physical therapy in the afternoon. Occupational therapy consisted of learning life skills. I would learn how to transition from the wheelchair to the mat table in a safe manner. Initially, I had to use a slide board to make the transition. Safety was very important. We went over small things like do not place your fingers in the door frame as you transition the wheelchair through the door, or you might pinch your fingers; always lock your wheelchair prior to standing up; and pop a wheelie to transition the wheelchair onto a curb. There are anti-tippers on the back of the wheelchair, which I had to learn to trust. Once I learned to trust the wheelchair's anti-tippers, I could pop a wheelie at will.

Other simple tasks would include lying flat on my stomach, arching up on my elbows, and then extending to the full range of my arm length. Having sat in the wheelchair so often, just positioning my body in the opposing direction was very painful. After I got a little stronger, I would play electronic games to help my balance.

Outpatient Rehabilitation

"Get up take your mat and go home."

Matthew 9:6

O
UTPATIENT REHABILITATION started with three sessions per week while in my wheelchair. Evelyn would take me to each session and stay for the duration. The therapist would have me walk up and down the stairs without holding onto the railing. Going up the stairs was not too bad but going down was psychologically scary. The therapist was small in stature but very knowledgeable on the mechanics of the body. I often wondered how such a slight of build guy was confident he could keep me (six feet, two inches) from falling if I lost my balance. I nicknamed him the Incredible Hulk because he knew just how to jerk the gate belt to make sure I regained my balance. I always wanted to impress my therapist. If it was a nice day, we would walk outside on grass, and uneven surfaces. I will never forget when he wanted me to cross a four-lane street at the stop light. My balance was not that great, so my gait was very slow. When that light turned red, I moved as fast as I could to reach the other side of the street. Yes, I trusted my therapist. My last session with the outpatient therapist was expected to end soon. To impress my therapist, I walked a five-kilometer Heart Mini Marathon in March 2015. It was the most difficult five-kilometer walk of my life, but I knew I was going to transition to the next chapter in my journey. I was the very last person to cross the finish line. There were cheerleaders

from a local school who hung around to energize those of us who brought up the rear of the marathon.

From August 2012 through March 2015, I worked very closely with doctors and therapists on a frequent basis. After graduating from the outpatient therapist, I still met with my primary care physician and the physical medicine rehabilitation doctor. My goal is to walk the Heart Mini Marathon every year.

Going Back to College

"We rejoice in our sufferings, knowing that suffering produces
endurance, and endurance produces character,
and character produces hope."

Romans 5:3–4

A FEW MONTHS AFTER returning home, I decided I wanted
to finish the master's degree in business administration that
I began in fall 2011. We had a meeting with the university admissions team, and we decided to take one class to start. Now, I will
be honest, I forgot how to use my calculator. Prior to taking my
first class, I needed to remember how to use my calculator. I also
needed a colleague and a friend, Bill, to help me figure out how
to use my smart phone. My wife was concerned but supportive.
My wife agreed that I could go back to college, but she did not
share with me that she was worried. She was worried only because
she did not know if my full mental capacity had returned. Evelyn
stayed in close contact with the college business office during
my illness. I initially signed up for just one finance class. Evelyn
would take me to school in my wheelchair and often wait in the
parking lot until my class was over. Because I was weak, Evelyn
would break down my wheelchair, pack it in the vehicle, reassemble it upon arrival, and wheel me to my class. For me, it was
important to finish what I started. I would attend class but did
not have great control of my faculties. It was not unusual for me
to soil myself while sitting in class. I remember one time I was
taking a test and sat in my waste while I completed the exam. I

wore adult diapers, so I was prepared. I had about halfway to go before I would graduate with my master's degree.

Right before my MBA graduation in winter 2014, classmates from my previous executive MBA class paid me a surprise visit after class. It was an emotional evening and will never forget that day.

As I continued to take classes, I graduated from the wheelchair to a walker to, eventually, a cane. I finally graduated with a master's degree in December 2014. I also got control of my bowels. I was determined to finish school.

I was excited that a local news station did a story about my illness, determination, and highlighted the *love* and support of Evelyn throughout the entire journey. I know Evelyn deserves an honorary diploma herself.

Protect Yourself

"But in your hearts honor Christ the Lord as holy, always being prepared to make a defense to anyone who asks you for a reason for the hope that is in you; yet do it with gentleness and respect."

1 Peter 3:15

I F THERE IS ONE THING that I want someone to take away from the experiences of my illness it would be to "use insect repellent." Just a few minutes of prevention is worth avoiding a lifetime of pain. Mosquitoes are known to be the most dangerous animals to humans. From malaria, chikungunya, yellow fever, and Zika, to name a few, the mosquito may be small but has a big impact. Wear long sleeves when outside in the brush and cutting the lawn.

Another Miracle

"For where two or three have gathered together in My name,
I am there in their midst."

Matthew 18:20

D URING MY ILLNESS, my wife, Evelyn, started attending a newly formed rosary group at the church. The small but powerful group would ask for various intentions at each *prayer* session. Although a large church, the rosary group was small— anywhere from eight to twelve people. Now for sure, Evelyn would ask for intentions for me each time she attended. One of the members of that rosary group worked in the business office of the business school where I was working on my MBA. When I had to drop out of my earlier MBA program, this individual was aware of my story due to the rosary group and my wife's intentions. Often when attending class at the university, there was an individual who said, "Hello, Jeffrey" each time I saw her. Now, I had been in a coma, and I did not have the courage to ask, "Who are you?" Approximately a year or so after I was discharged from the hospital, I attended the rosary group at our church myself. My wife stated that there was a person in the rosary group who works at the university. Well, we met that night, and for me, it was a full-circle moment. It is hard for me to express my humility knowing that this group was praying for me. It was miraculous that one of the members of that small Rosary group worked in the very department where I was receiving my master's degree.

Some Tips for Helping Those with a Physical Disability

I LEARNED A GREAT DEAL being in a disabled state. I tried to remember a few to share here.

- First, you may think you are doing a person a favor by buying them furniture or aids to support their disability, but I would caution you to think twice. One recommendation I have is to try it out for yourself first. If you are able-bodied and have difficulty sitting in a small shower chair (for example) or bedside commode, imagine having a disability and doing the same thing. Sit in the chair and see if it feels stable. I, personally, like the tub side chair/bench; it feels much steadier for me. Also, for me to take a shower, I first had to transition from my wheelchair to a shower chair outside the shower, and then to the tub-side bench in the shower. It literally took me five hours to complete a shower; I could barely lift my leg a few inches off the ground. I was initially encouraged to build a ramp into the shower.

- Also, before taking the doors off the hinges to accommodate the wheelchair, carefully see if the wheelchair can fit.

For many weeks, I had curtains on my bedroom and bathroom doors.

- Also, if a bedside commode is needed, a good tip is to use small plastic trash bags or plastic grocery store bags to line the inside of the bedside commode before each use. The cleanup is quick and easy.

- I highly recommend getting long-term insurance if it is available. In some cases, this type of insurance will pay a percentage of your salary for the period of time you are out of work.

- Have relentless *faith* and steadfast *prayer*. *Pray* often.

- Move, if only a little each day. I was often reminded of the person in my neighborhood who I would see walking around the block every now and then. This individual has muscular dystrophy and was not able to walk upright. He would walk slowly but steadily around the block utilizing a cane. I was told that walking helps to discourage the muscles from seizing up.

- Ensure you have an advocate for the patient in the hospital. It is important for someone to recount what happened. It helps to fill in the blanks when things start to settle down.

- Listen to your body. No one knows your body better than you. Please do not be a hero.

- Adult diapers are your friend. Adult diapers are readily available. They can be a little pricey, though. I recommend placing an additional pad inside and do not remove the pad's protective cover. We often wear adult diapers that are tight enough to hold the pad in place. This way, when the pad gets wet, you can remove it and dispose of it and then replace it with a fresh pad. You remain (sort of) dry. I do not like to walk around with a soggy adult diaper. Keep extra pads in your pocket or purse.

- If you are the caregiver for a disabled or elderly person, there are government agencies that can help. I like the Counsel for Aging, which has offices in many locations.

- Beware of mattresses that are too soft. My pillow-top mattress was nice when I had a strong core; however, when I lost 30 percent of my body weight and had little core strength, I sank into that pillow top mattress and could not turn over. Fortunately, we had a firm mattress in a spare room.

- Label your walker, wheelchair, and canes with peelable address labels. I found they often fade and need replacement, but labels can quickly let people at work and church know where to return your item.

- Don't wait until you have a major illness to tell your partner you *love* him or her. Life is short, why not enjoy every moment?

There are many more golden nuggets I learned along the way. I will have to capture them all and possibly summarize in another book. I found that spending a few more dollars was worth it.

A Wife's Perspective

"She will do him good and not evil all the days of her life."

Proverbs 31:12

I T WAS AUGUST 2012, and I was excited and looking forward to my planned trip to Cleveland for a Pediatric Board Review course at the Cleveland Clinic. It was not unusual for Jeffrey to travel globally more than 100,000 miles per year in his role at work. Yes, I was excited to learn new things and focus on me for a change. It was an important year because I had to renew my Pediatric Boards. I had fallen behind in my preparation for the upcoming exam. There were sure to be insightful comments from colleagues about a variety of topics. Of course, the social part of the visit was a draw as well. I was looking forward to reconnecting with my friends who I had not seen for many years.

The day of the trip, Jeffrey had a fever. His temperature measured from 100.4 to 101 degrees Fahrenheit. He looked sick but not any sicker than someone with a mild viral issue. I did not like the combination of an adult and fever. I felt like I should stay home, but Jeffrey insisted that I travel to Cleveland and enjoy myself, as it was only one week. Jeffrey reassured me that he would be fine and could manage everything. I left with trepidation as I had never seen Jeffrey ill except for the cluster headaches. I taught our son what changes in his dad to look for (i.e., increased sleepiness, headaches, vomiting, not eating, or confusion). Our son was my eyes and ears while I was gone. I instructed our son to keep an eye on his dad and call me about any changes in his condition. I knew I could trust him because he was dependable.

<u>Day One at the Conference</u>: Jeffrey told me he ate some chicken noodle soup and drank plenty of liquids. His temperature went up slightly to 102 degrees Fahrenheit. I instructed Jeffrey that he should go to the emergency room because I was concerned that he had something serious going on.

Jeffrey went to the emergency room. I called one of my contacts at the hospital to look out for him. I was concerned he might have the West Nile virus, as I recalled Jeffrey shared that he saw dead birds in the yard a few weeks before.

The emergency room doctor felt Jeffrey did not have meningitis, so he treated him with intravenous (IV) fluids and discharged him to go home with a pain medication prescription.

<u>Day Two at the Conference</u>: I went to the conference thinking Jeffrey would turn around. Knowing he did not have meningitis was good, and he would be just fine. The first day of lectures were very interesting—and retrospectively, they were enlightening. The lecture topics were fluids, electrolytes, and management of Syndrome of Inappropriate Anitdiaretic Hormone Secretion (SDAH), renal insufficiency—all topics that I had not seen in a while because of my long time in out-patient settings where these topics rarely existed.

<u>Day Three at the Conference</u>: I called home and discovered Jeffrey was sleeping a lot that evening and not eating well, but he was drinking his fluids. When Jeffrey and I spoke, he seemed coherent. He continued to encourage me to stay at the pediatric conference. I told him that I think I needed to come home. His fever was now between 102 and 103 degrees Fahrenheit.

<u>Later That Day at the Conference</u>: I became more and more concerned and made the decision to go home and not visit with my friends. I made the drive home in record time. During the

entire trip, I was hoping Jeffrey did not have bacterial meningitis, which is very deadly. When I arrived home, Jeffrey looked very ill, but he was trying to put on a good show for me. He was singing and dancing. I looked in the refrigerator and saw five uneaten bowls of chicken noodle soup. He had stopped eating due to a lack of appetite.

<u>Day One Back Home</u>: The next morning, Jeffrey said his head and spine hurt. After taking our son to school, I took Jeffrey to the emergency room. Jeffrey was interested in what the insurance deductible would be for this emergency room visit. I thought to myself, "Are you kidding me?"

Evelyn stated, "The overall cost would be the same as a new car, but you are worth it." Once we arrived at the emergency room, I dropped Jeffrey off at the front door. He walked into the emergency room. I sat in the car for several minutes, saying lots of *prayers* because I knew he had meningitis and how serious it could be.

Also, it was August, and as a previous teaching physician, I knew it was the time of the year the new residents had only been working one month or so. I prayed that I would know what to do, recognize any problems, and have the confidence to know that I could support this with God's grace. I was smart, and he was determined that he would not leave the emergency room with only a diagnosis of the flu.

Jeffrey was ill, and the hospital staff took him to the back and gave him a room right away. The emergency room (ER) doctor was a parishioner from our church. We were familiar with each other because our kids had attended elementary school together at Saint Mary Hyde Park. I was relieved because I felt that God was sending me messages to calm down! The ER doctor did Jeffrey's spinal tap and ordered all the appropriate labs.

I called Jeffrey's colleague from work and let him know what was going on.

Final Thoughts

AFTER BUGGING MY WIFE FOR MONTHS, if not years, to share her specific and detailed insights about my illness, I finally realized that those memories were painful for her to remember.

Sometimes people say I did not get the outcome I wanted, but maybe I got the outcome I needed. I know that everyone who observed me go from a wheelchair to a walker to a cane can't help but believe in the power of our Holy Spirit and the resilience of the human spirit. I am a walking testimony without even talking.

I don't think science and God are separate—they go together. Science sometimes answers the "how" but rarely or never tells you the "why" if you question phenomenon to the void. You can say how the mosquito infected me, but when you ask questions into the void, it does not explain the "how."

God is good all the time!

E-mails Received During My Illness

Sent: Monday, September 10, 2012, 12:47 PM
Subject: FW: Jeff Daniel update

Evelyn would like to take this opportunity to thank all of you for your support during this trying time. At this juncture, the Daniel family respectfully requests no visitors at the hospital as they work towards Jeff's full recovery. Your continued prayers are invaluable, and I will keep you all informed as developments occur.

Jeff is resting comfortably. His doctors feel he is heading in the right direction. Evelyn, and the children are also doing much better.

Once she understands the full scope of his recovery, she will reach out, and we can jump in.

Again, please keep Jeff and his family in your prayers

Had a great day yesterday... moving arms freely and upon command, clearly recognizes activity around him, sat up on side of bed with help, and wiggled his toes

Keep those prayers coming.

Sent: Friday, September 14, 2012, 11:36 AM
Subject: FW: Jeff update

Happy Friday! Please find the below

Additionally, ... visited with Jeff until 9pm last night and felt very encouraged by Jeff's responses and engagement :)

Please continue praying, this is all Jeff and his family have asked for.

Thanks so much.

Sent: Tuesday, September 18, 2012, 3:06 PM
Subject: RE: Jeff update

Just a quick note to let you know that people remain encouraged by Jeff's continued progress :) So good to hear.

Thanks for everyone's continued prayers.

Sent: Thursday, September 20, 2012, 12:45 PM
Subject: Jeff update

All, more good news!!!! Jeff is now breathing on his own through a trach. He appears stronger during physical therapy.

Please keep him in your prayers...

Sent: Thursday, September 20, 2012, 1:07 PM
Subject: RE: Jeff update

The latest is below, and it continues to be All Good!! Please continue praying for Jeff per his family's requests.

Some of Jeff's first verbal words were — When can I Eat??!! :)
Another great sign.

Sent: Friday, September 21, 2012, 12:41 PM
Subject: RE: Jeff update

Jeff's wife, Evelyn reached out today!! Jeff wanted to share that
he is getting better, he is recovering, and he is preparing for Rehab
at this time!!

Jeff & Evelyn are most thankful for everyone's prayers. The
journey is not over but he is well on the way :)

We saw another good sign of Jeff's improvement in that last night
he was blaming Kofi for his illness. All's well :)

Happy Friday! (*Under*statement.)

Sent: Monday, September 24, 2012, 2:27 PM
Subject: RE: Jeff update

Progress continues. Jeff is settling in at Rehab at this time. This is
a tremendous step. Please pray for his continued quality care and
protection at this new facility.

Most appreciated.

Sent: Wednesday, September 26, 2012, 12:36 PM
Subject: RE: Jeff update

Thank you so much for keeping us posted on Jeff's condition. It is so
nice to know Jeff's family has the support they need. God is good!

Peace,

Jeffrey A. Daniel

Sent: Friday, September 28, 2012, 12:58 PM
Subject: RE: Jeff update

Happy Friday to all! The Jeff reports are continuing positively! He is actively engaged in all his therapies and always striving to hit those stretch goals :) Evelyn's finding that very amusing.

Your prayers are very effective and sustaining him and his family more than you could ever imagine.

On Fri, Sep 28, 2012, at 2:05 PM:

Hi everyone, Evelyn has asked me to help facilitate Jeff's expanding visitor rotation :) In particular she is greatly thankful for positive friends who can uplift and/or fire up Jeff through these Rehab weeks :)

She asks that everyone please be mindful of their own good health. Please reach out to this Distribution if you would need a back-up if you are experiencing symptoms of any kind or if something personal arises--thank you!!

Evelyn is still maintaining 1 Visitor per day at present and during the following hours:

- Monday-Friday 6-8PM
- Saturday-Sunday 4-6PM

Evelyn also appreciates everyone respecting Jeff's privacy and confidentiality around his condition—thanks

Jeff and Evelyn are most appreciative of your time and great support to their family.

Thank you!

Sent: Monday, October 01, 2012, 4:00 PM
Subject: RE: Good Samaritan Rehab - Jeff's VISITOR Schedule

Evelyn says the ventilator is now out of Jeff's room :)

Sent: Monday, October 01, 2012, 4:24 PM
Subject: RE: Jeff update

Continued strong progress. Jeff's breathing only room air at this point – fully weaned from O_2 :)

Great things. Please continue praying and encouraging; it means everything.

Sent: Monday, October 01, 2012, 5:56 PM
Subject: RE: Jeff update

Thanks, great news!! Prayer is powerful and we will keep lifting Jeff up in prayer.

Sent: Thursday, October 04, 2012, 10:59 AM
Subject: RE: Jeff update

More great gains! Jeff is eating regular hospital food and working on his physical strength—this will take time. He has his humor. When someone commented on his good-looking turkey burger, he said... "Do you want it?" :) Jeff's words to all were: "Thanks for your thoughts and prayers. Have a great week."

... Thanks for your continued prayers. Jeff is so anxious to be strong enough to go home.

Sent: Thursday, October 04, 2012, 11:06 AM
Subject: RE: Jeff update

Excellent! Evelyn texted me last night and said his trach had been reducebd in size and capped, so all breathing through nose/mouth only.

Sent: Friday, October 05, 2012, 11:49 AM
Subject: RE: Jeff update

Hi everyone,... you will enjoy this one for your Happy and Funny Friday :)

Jeff is completely <u>trach-free</u>... by his own accord. Yes, the trach had been reduced in size and the staff was working towards removal (in a few more days to a week) but it was itching and bothering Jeff... so, *he removed it* yesterday. The staff decided it would not need to be replaced :)

That's our Jeff.

On behalf of Jeff & Evelyn, thanks for keeping him in thought and prayer.

Sent: Monday, October 08, 2012, 5:04 PM
Subject: RE: Jeff update

Jeff's great strides continue. He is working very hard to regain strength and spent time this weekend pushing himself/his wheelchair up and down his long hallway. Apparently, this action is not common on this specific rehab floor and caused quite a stir. Other patients saw Jeff wheeling around and began asking the staff for the same opportunity :)

And now Jeff is preparing to move to the rehab floor intended for more extensive therapy!

Please remember and pray for Jeff as he takes on new and greater challenges this week!

Sent: Wednesday, October 10, 2012, 10:29 AM
Subject: RE: Jeff update

Jeff has successfully moved therapy floors as planned and is scheduled this morning for 4 hours of extensive therapy. He will be rigorously challenged.

I wanted to share his wife's personal request...

Please continue to pray for Jeff, to see signs of success every day and that he is filled with Hope and optimism as he works towards a full and complete recovery.

Thank you, Evelyn

Let's lift up Jeff during this monumental challenge! It makes all the difference.
Thank you,

Sent: Monday, October 22, 2012, 2:50 PM
Subject: RE: Jeff update - Prayer

Jeff's progress in rehab is substantial; he has a packed schedule from 7AM–4PM for varied therapies and his demeanor is great.

Evelyn just reached out for prayers regarding clotting in Jeff's legs. He is undergoing surgery within the hour to insert a filter within his inferior vena cava ...

Although Evelyn calls the situation a minor setback, please take a moment to pray for Jeff and all his caregivers at this time.

Sent: Monday, October 22, 2012, 5:08 PM
Subject: RE: Jeff update - Prayer

From Evelyn Daniel:

"Procedure went extremely well. Perfect position of filter. No complications. Jeff is resting comfortably. Thank you for the prayers!"

Add prayers of thanks!

Sent: Monday, October 29, 2012 ,4:08 PM
Subject: RE: Jeff update - Prayer

Jeff's doing great. Just wanted to share this as a little reminder. I asked Jeff today if there's anything special we can get for him.

Jeff's response, "I am good. I just need your continued prayers."

He and Evelyn are steadfast in their wishes :)

Thanks to all.

Sent: Tuesday, October 30, 2012, 2:18 PM
Subject: RE: Jeff update - Prayer

Hello again, saw Jeffrey last night and he is really well. His legs remain his greatest challenge. By all other accounts I am sure he has had enough of the hospital, but he clearly stated:

"It is not important to me to get home as fast as possible. It is important to me to recover."

He also said, "I hope my spirit stays strong for the duration."

We know what to pray for. He is working very hard, working to enable his legs to fully bear his weight. Please keep Jeff close in thought and prayer.

Sent: Tuesday, October 30, 2012, 3:17 PM
Subject: RE: Jeff update - Prayer

Will continue to bombard the gates of heaven with prayers for his absolute recovery. Thanks for sharing specifics.

Sent: Wednesday, December 05, 2012, 12:21 PM
Subject: RE: Jeffrey Daniel Update - Prayer ~ GOING HOME!!!
Importance: High

All,
Just as Jeff had hoped for and planned, I just learned this morning that he is being released to Go Home on Friday!! Evelyn and he and all are thrilled! :) He will continue with outpatient therapies.

With all sincerity, *thank you* for all the prayers...

Sent: Friday, November 09, 2012, 4:49 PM
Subject: RE: Jeff update - Prayer

Hi to all and Happy Friday :)

I wanted to share that I'm continuing to hear all good things about Jeff... high spirits, a determined will for full recovery, and steady daily and weekly progress. Jeff's therapy is demanding, and he is All In. With assistance he is getting up on his legs and making them work for him in Therapy. Occupationally he and his family are working on movements from his chair to a vehicle, etc.

Jeff sends his sincere thanks for keeping him in thought and prayer. God bless him.

Sent: Wednesday, November 28, 2012, 9:58 AM
Subject: Jeffrey Daniel Update - Prayer

Hello All,
I spoke to Jeff yesterday afternoon, and he sounds great! He remains very spirited!

Although he wasn't feeling up for a day pass on Thanksgiving, he did make it home for a Sunday afternoon visit.

The previous week some … associates visited as a team for lunch-time Friday, NOV 16. It was especially exciting for those who had not seen Jeff but of course *he* was most thrilled of all :)

His therapists are amping up his daily therapies more and more. With the support of braces/walker he has been able to walk 40–50 feet!! The new regimen is really fatiguing him, and he feels like he needs greater rest in the evenings, so he is now preferring his quiet to visitors :)

Jeff will not be Admitted much longer! He is waiting for the arrival of a new type of leg braces and then needs time to adapt to them and have them individually adjusted for him.

He is getting there!!!

Jeff is far beyond thankful for your many prayers and good wishes for him. These have been truly instrumental to his remarkable progress and recovery.

Per the Daniels' personal wishes expressed every time we speak, please continue to pray for Jeff's speedy and complete recovery. *This means everything* to him and his family.

Sent: Wednesday, December 05, 2012, 1:21 PM
Subject: RE: Jeffrey Daniel Update - Prayer ~ GOING HOME!!!

I have those Holy Spirit chills...!

Sent: Wednesday, December 05, 2012, 12:21 PM
Subject: RE: Jeffrey Daniel Update - Prayer ~ GOING HOME!!!
Importance: High

All,
Just as Jeff had hoped for and planned, I just learned this morning that he is being released to Go Home on Friday!! Evelyn and he and all are thrilled! :) He will continue with outpatient therapies.

With all sincerity, *thank you* for all the prayers...
(...personally, I think he's looking for greater comforts to watch the Army – Navy game Saturday...! ☺)

RE: Jeffrey Daniel Update — Back to Work!
Sent: Monday, February 25, 2013 6:47 PM
Subject: RE: Jeffrey Daniel Update

All—I wanted to share if you have not heard that you may very well have a Jeffrey Daniel sighting this week or certainly soon!... pls feel free to share with other business partners that work with Jeffrey, so they are aware.

Starting with an adjusted schedule, Jeffrey is returning to work this week :) ...

He will also continue his physical therapy regimen; this will seemingly be a long-term process.

Jeff has been eager to start; this week has been long-awaited. Let's be mindful of the many adjustments he will be undergoing as he transitions back, just all the faces alone will be a lot.

I know his focus is on the future and where he is going and not what happened or what he has been through—it would be good to let Jeff direct that part of any conversation if he wants rather than asking. It's difficult repeating things and some unanswered questions will always remain, even for Jeff and his family.

Thank you for your continued support and prayers as Jeff undergoes this great environmental transition. He has missed his work family very much and he is forever grateful for your unending prayers and support that sustained him and his family through his challenge.

Thank you,

Sent: Monday, March 16, 2015, 4:48 PM
Subject: 1008-10302012

... no better time than Lent as a reminder of your and His great sacrifices for the saving of souls. We are told by the saints of how just our humble acceptance of life's trials rescues holy souls from purgatory and how we can unite our suffering to His to bring even more souls to Him, especially those who will not save themselves. He wants *every soul,* and you are helping Him in His mission by your faithful witness!!!

God bless you and warmest congratulations. You are a true inspiration.

Likewise, your marriage is a blessed witness to the world! A shared Faith. Wherever two or more are gathered in His Name. Every single time you pray together, Jesus is there With You no matter where you are!

There is nothing greater—it's no wonder you are moving mountains!

————————————

Some Favorite Memories and Quotes

- Mosquitoes are the most dangerous animals to humans.
  o Seriously–this is true!
- Walking is overrated.
  o What I would say to my colleagues as I rode my scooter down the hallway.
- My name is Faith
  o The aesthetician who cheered my wife during a stressful moment.
- With Dr. Wunder and Mr. Miracle, I knew everything would be okay.
  o Enough said.
- Praying the rosary.
  o Comforted my wife during trying of times.
- Please pray for me at the wailing wall
  o I asked a friend from Israel to have a special prayer.
- Walking on borrowed braces for the first time
  o Standing on a hero's braces gave me great faith and inner strength.
- Attitude is everything
  o God is good – always!
- My wife falling asleep on my hospital bed
  o Her unconditional love was apparent to all.
- I don't recommend tube feeding as a weight-loss program
  o Be careful what you ask for...

- I do what I do, and you do what you do ...
  - o Let's do the best we can in our own lanes.
- A pillow-top mattress is very soft
  - o I'm slowly sinking and cannot get up!
- We should biopsy his brain ...
  - o What my wife overheard a doctor saying as I lay in a coma.
- Therapists are special people.
  - o They make each individual feel special—no matter what your background is..."
- Therapists and nurses are very special and have a special place in my heart.
- If that's the worst thing that happens to me today, then I think I am doing pretty well God is good.
- Nurse from Lima, Ohio, prayed for me every day
  - o I love Lima!
- Tall kneeling was tough—I needed it to pray.
  - o Tall kneeling prepared me for lots of prayer in the future.
- I am a walking evangelist for God.
  - o God is good!
- Ordinary people doing extraordinary things!
  - o I am inspired by the dedication and love of therapists.
- I must accept that I am a miracle.
  - o I cannot deny God's *love*, mercy, and grace.
- Strangers come up and share the encouragement I provided them.
  - o I must accept my role.
- Short term disability and American Express - He's baaack!
  - o I am accountable...
- I wrote, "I can't talk," to which my friend wrote, "I know."
  - o This was obvious for all involved.

- West Nile virus and the exact same vehicles
  - o   Another church member and I have a 1996 blue Toyota.
- From a wheelchair to a walker and a walker to a cane was significant; from a cane to independently walking was a big step."
- The journey continues... thanks for the love
- I'm looking forward to my continual walk with God.
- My wife's *love, faith and prayer* paved the way for miraculous results

Attitude is everything.

Live in the moment and trust God.

Yesterday is gone. Tomorrow is yet to come. Live for this day.

> *"It shall come to pass that before they call, I will answer; And while they are still speaking, I will hear."*
>
> Isaiah 65: 24

> *"Lord, it's easy to let discouragement sap my energy and joy. Help me to reject all agents of discouragement in my life and to trust in You for comfort and strength."*
>
> DD For March 2, 2015
> Our Daily Bread—A Deadly Weapon

> *"For I will restore health to you and heal you of your wounds, says the Lord."*
>
> Jeremiah 30:17